SONG, SPEECH,
AND
VENTRILOQUISM

SONG, SPEECH,
AND
VENTRILOQUISM

written and illustrated by
LARRY KETTELKAMP

William Morrow and Company
New York 1967

To my wife, Florence,
whose joy is song
and whose song is life.

CONTENTS

YOUR VOICE IS YOU

Whether you use your voice for singing, for speaking or for mimicry and imitation, it is a combination of mind and body. All of us make sounds with the same basic muscles. But no two bodies are ever alike, no two personalities are ever alike, and every voice is different from all others.

Most of the muscles and cartilages that are used to produce vocal sounds lie inside the body. Many belong to the group of muscles that work for you automatically as you breathe, swallow, cough, or yawn. Since you do not have to think about doing these things, they are called reflex actions. They are really reactions. If your lungs are empty, you

11

react by breathing in air. When you place food at the back of your throat, you react by swallowing. When something irritates your windpipe, you cough. When you need a large amount of oxygen quickly, you yawn. All of these things happen automatically.

Your voice is part of this reflex system. The wish to say something to another person causes all of the needed muscular actions. You do not have to decide which muscles to use. You probably do not feel your muscles working at all. You can control consciously some of the movements of your tongue, lips, jaw, and large breathing muscles. But you are not aware of most of the smaller muscles in your throat. And when you are speaking or singing, you feel nothing at all. Everything is working by reflex.

Some reflex actions, such as sighing, starting to yawn, or laughing are helpful to the voice. They make it sound clearer and more pleasant. And if you are relaxed or happy, your voice automatically reflects these feelings. It sounds stronger, and your words will be more easily understood. Other reflex actions hinder your voice. If you are frightened or embarrassed, reflexes such as swallowing, closing your mouth, or holding your breath may partly block your voice and make it sound weaker. Sometimes these reflexes may even stop the sound completely. Have you ever been speechless when you were suddenly surprised?

This relation of your voice to your personality is why your voice is you.

HOW YOUR VOICE WORKS

Your voice has three important parts: the bellows, the vibrator, and the resonators. The bellows extend from your collarbone down to your hips. The vibrator is inside your Adam's apple. The resonators are your throat, mouth, and sometimes your nose. Thus, you use a large part of your body when you use your voice. However, these parts of your anatomy have other functions as well.

The Bellows

At the base of your throat hangs a tube called the trachea, which means *rough*. Rings of cartilage make this tube look something like the hose of a vacuum sweeper. The trachea splits into two

14

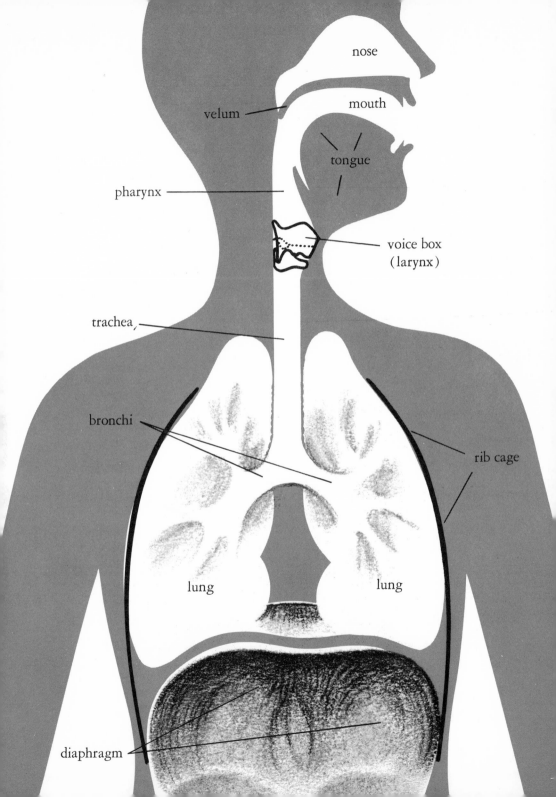

smaller tubes called the bronchi, meaning *wind-pipes*. The bronchi in turn split off into a mass of tubes that become smaller. They form the lungs —two spongy masses that fill most of the chest cavity. The rib cage surrounds the lungs.

Stretching across the base of the rib cage is a large muscle shaped something like an upside-down bowl. It is called the diaphragm, which means *divider,* and it separates the chest cavity from the lower body cavity. When the diaphragm tightens, the middle part moves down, and it becomes flat like a dinner plate. In this position it makes the chest cavity larger, and air rushes in to fill the space. When it relaxes it returns to its humped-up shape, gently pushing out the used air. Normally the action of the diaphragm is automatic.

Below the diaphragm are most of your inside organs. And around them are overlapping walls of muscles. Those at the front and sides make a group called abdominal muscles, meaning *of the belly.*

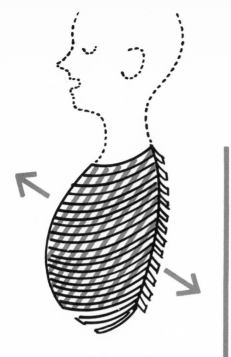

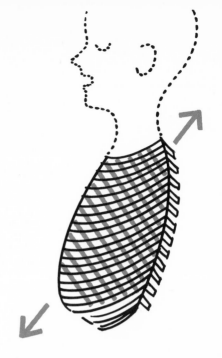

Muscles between ribs lift and expand chest.

Opposing muscles between ribs collapse chest.

There are also muscles that fit between the ribs in a crisscross pattern. One set pulls the rib cage into a flatter shape, like that of a cardboard box pushed askew. They make the space inside smaller. The other set pulls the rib cage back, as if they were straightening the sides of the squashed box. They increase the inside space.

When a person is breathing or talking quietly, the diaphragm may do most of the work. When he is singing, talking loudly, or shouting, the chest and abdominal muscles are used as well. When the abdominals contract they flatten, pushing against the organs inside the lower body cavity. This squeeze exerts an upward pressure on the diaphragm. If the diaphragm relaxes, the abdominals will push it quickly back into its humped-up position. At the same time the air is

inhale   exhale

BREATH CONTROL

Chest is gently expanded.
Diaphragm tightens and
flattens. Abdominals
tighten in opposition.
A bulge appears below
rib cage. Diaphragm
relaxes gradually as
abdominals increase
tension. Stomach
flattens as breath
is exhaled. Chest
feels expanded as at
first until a new
breath is taken.

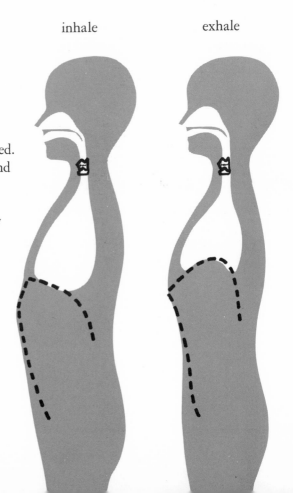

forced out of the lungs in a sharp blast. An ordinary cough uses some of this action.

The whole body is made up of groups of muscles that oppose each other. For instance, contracting the muscles on one side of the arm makes it bend. Contracting those on the other side makes it extend. Tightening both groups locks your arm in a fixed position. In the same way the diaphragm opposes the abdominal muscles. If you take a breath and hold it, you tighten your diaphragm. Now if you tighten your abdominal muscles, but do not relax your diaphragm, you are setting some of the largest opposing muscles of your body against each other. In the strength of these opposing muscles lies the secret of what a singer or a stage actor calls breath control.

The Vibrator

Above the bellows section is the voice box. At the top of the trachea is a circle of cartilage called the cricoid, which means *ring*. It is higher at the back than at the front, like a signet ring. Just above and arching around the front is the thyroid cartilage. Thyroid means *shield-shaped*. If you hold the palms of your hands a few inches apart and touch the tips of your last three fingers together, you will make a shape like that of the double shields of the thyroid cartilage. These cartilages, the cricoid and the thyroid, form the voice box called the larynx.

Inside the larynx are the vocal cords. They are a pair of muscles in the shape of thick lips about an inch long, and they run from front to back. Where the edges meet, the cords are thinner. At the front the cords come together in the pointed V of the thyroid cartilage. This projection is what we call the Adam's apple. On either side at the back are two small cartilages called arytenoids, meaning *ladle-shaped*. They rock out and in over the edges of the cricoid ring. The vocal cords are attached to these cartilages. When the arytenoids rock up and apart, the cords are parted at the back

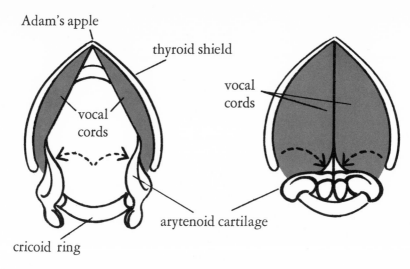

Adam's apple

thyroid shield

vocal
cords

vocal
cords

arytenoid cartilage

cricoid ring

THE LARYNX SEEN FROM ABOVE
At left the arytenoid cartilages rock out over
the cricoid ring to open the throat for a breath.
At right the arytenoids rock inward to bring
the vocal cords together ready to vibrate.

and leave a V-shaped opening. Small muscles can
rock these cartilages together in several ways, thus
closing the gap between the vocal cords.

The thyroid shields also rock against the cricoid
ring at two pivot points on the sides. Muscles attached between the thyroid and the cricoid can
tense, causing the thyroid cartilage to rock forward and down. This movement stretches the
vocal cords tighter and makes them a little longer.
The cords themselves also contain muscles. When

21

they are tensed they act in the opposite way, shortening the cords a little.

The vocal cords form a sort of mouth inside your throat. Often this mouth is simply opened and closed like a valve. It is closed when you swallow, so that food does not drop down the trachea. In addition, it is covered by a leaf-shaped cartilage, called the epiglottis, at the back of your tongue. It covers your voice box like a lid when you swallow. When you lift something heavy, you take a deep breath and close your vocal cords, so that your abdominal muscles have something to press against. If the valve slips open a little, you may grunt as you lift. When you cough, you first close the valve tightly, then blast it open with air pushed out by your abdominal muscles.

The vocal cords can be vibrated with a flow of air to create the sounds you use in speech and singing. When the valve is nearly closed and the bellows force a stream of air between the vocal cords, the air is squeezed through the slit faster than it moves in the wider spaces above and

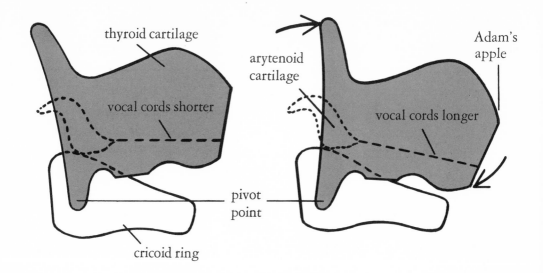

thyroid cartilage

arytenoid cartilage

Adam's apple

vocal cords shorter

vocal cords longer

pivot point

cricoid ring

Muscles can pivot thyroid cartilage
forward and down to stretch vocal cords
longer and thinner, helping to raise pitch.

below the gap. The fast-moving air becomes less dense, and the vocal cords are sucked together. Once the gap is closed, air pressure builds up until it forces the cords apart again, and a puff of air escapes. These puffs of air are released many times per second. Their frequency ranges from fewer than 100 times per second up to more than 1000 times per second. The more frequent the puffs, the higher the sound.

A sound something like that made by the vocal cords can also be made with your outside lips.

23

The player of a trumpet or any of the brass instruments uses it to produce the tone he wants. First, smile until the muscles at the corners of your mouth become very firm. At the same time, bring your lips as close together as you can without touching. Purse your stretched lips a little like the start of a kiss. Now force a very strong stream of air between your lips. They will be sucked together and will vibrate with a tingling sensation. If they are firmly stretched and held in about the same position, you should be able to make a tone something like a mixture of a buzz and a hum. The tighter and thinner your lips, the higher the hum. The thicker and looser they are, the lower the hum. If you had no throat and no head, your voice would sound in much this way.

Two more experiments can help to illustrate the action of the bellows and the vibrator. First, sit down. Blow up a balloon. Tuck it gently between your knees. Pinch the neck on both sides with the thumb and first finger of each hand, and stretch the neck a little by moving your hands slightly apart. As the air rushes out of the balloon it causes the stretched rubber sides of the neck to vibrate, making a sound like that of a very high voice. The relaxation of the balloon is a little like the relaxation of the diaphragm. The sides of the neck vibrate in somewhat the same way as the vocal cords do when the air rushes past them.

Since the balloon is tucked between your knees, you can keep the air pressure steady for a while, as it collapses, by gently squeezing the balloon. The more the balloon collapses, the harder you

Blow up balloon. Place between knees. Pinch neck between thumb and finger of each hand. Escaping air vibrates the sides of the neck. As balloon collapses knees increase pressure to keep steady flow of air.

will have to squeeze to keep the air pressure steady. This squeeze is a little like the inward pressure of the abdominal muscles that helps push the breath out smoothly. You will discover that the balloon neck must be gently and steadily stretched and that the air pressure must be kept firm and even in order to make the tone sound musical. The muscles of your body must perform just as well if you want to use your voice as a musical instrument.

For the second experiment you will need two sheets of tablet or typing paper. Pinch one sheet between the thumb and forefinger of your right

Blow down between two sheets of paper. The breath stream sucks them together and they vibrate.

hand, and the other in your left. Let them hang so there is just a little space between the sheets. Blow a strong and steady stream of air down between the sheets of paper. The fast-moving air is less dense than the still air pressing on the other side of each sheet. The sheets of paper will be sucked together and will vibrate. This sucking action is similar to the one that causes the vocal cords to vibrate.

The Resonators

Just above the vocal cords lie two smaller wedges of muscle called the false vocal cords. The base of the tongue is attached to a bone above the false cords.

The tongue is a remarkable muscle that can make itself into just about any shape that there is room for. When it lies flat in your mouth, it leaves an open space shaped rather like an upside-down letter J. The space between the base of the tongue and the back of the throat is called the pharynx, and, of course, the mouth is the space that curves forward. By humping up in the middle, the tongue can divide the two inside spaces in many ways, leaving a narrow passage between them. It can make a large pharynx and a small mouth or vice versa. It can also make the two spaces about the same size.

The roof of the mouth is made of hard cartilage covered with only a thin layer of skin. To the rear of the roof is a small muscular flap called the velum. It forms the arched shape you see when you look in the mirror and say *ah*. The sides of this flap, which are called pillars, run down and beneath the tongue. The velum can be lifted to touch the back of the throat or dropped forward. When it is dropped forward, it opens a passage into the nose above. The nose is full of narrow winding passages of soft tissue with many hairs. These passages warm the air you breathe and trap dust and other particles as they enter. When speaking or singing, you may use almost any combination of the throat, mouth, and nose cavi-

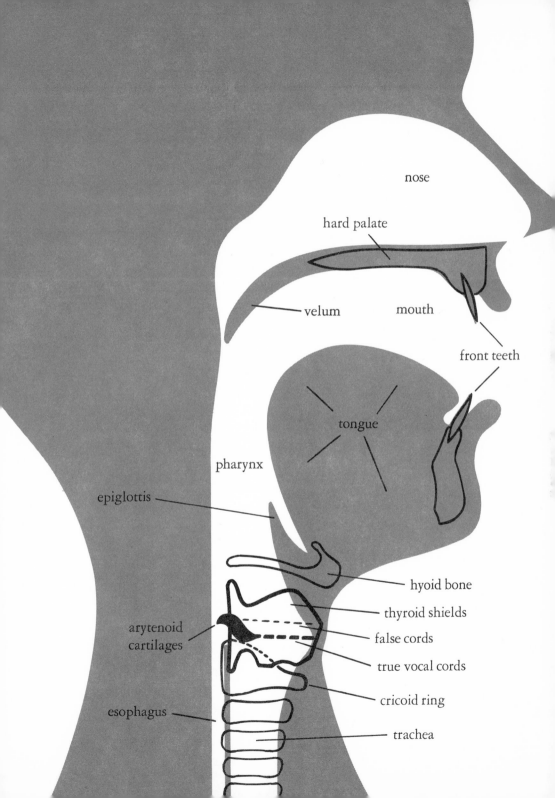

nose

hard palate

velum

mouth

front teeth

tongue

pharynx

epiglottis

hyoid bone

thyroid shields

arytenoid cartilages

false cords

true vocal cords

cricoid ring

esophagus

trachea

ties to change the sounds that are made by the vocal cords.

Any enclosed cavity holds a certain volume of air. If the air inside is set into vibration, it sounds a tone of its own. The smaller the cavity, the higher the tone. Also the material that encloses the cavity may affect the sound. And if the cavity has a small opening, its sound will be lower than if it has a large opening.

An experiment with a pop bottle can illustrate the vibrations of a cavity of air. Blow gently across the top of an empty bottle. The air inside will vibrate, making a rather low tone. Put a little water in the bottle and blow again. The tone will be higher because the remaining air space is smaller and vibrates more frequently. Each time you add more water the air cavity becomes smaller and the pitch rises. The sound becomes more and more like that of a high whistle. In fact, you do the same thing with your tongue as you whistle. Whistle a low note, and then slide the pitch up. In order to do so, you move your tongue forward toward your teeth leaving a smaller and smaller air cavity at the front of your mouth.

Another easy experiment will show how the size of the opening affects the pitch of the cavity. All you need is an ordinary teaspoon. Open your mouth as if you were going to say *ah*. Using the bottom of the spoon as a little hammer, gently tap your cheek on the soft fleshy part. The air inside your mouth will produce a dull tone. Keep tapping your cheek and gradually close your lips and round them. Try to keep the inside of your mouth in about the same position by holding your jaw steady. As your mouth opening becomes

smaller the pitch of your mouth cavity becomes lower. After a little practice you can play a tune with the spoon merely by moving your lips.

Any two objects or cavities that vibrate at the same pitch are said to be resonant, which means *to sound again.* When the air in the first cavity is set into vibration, the second cavity will also vibrate if it is nearby. When you push someone in a swing, you know that you must push at just the right time in order to increase the motion of the swing. If you push at the wrong time, the swing bumps and slows down. But if you push a little every time the swing starts to move away from you, you can easily keep the swing in motion for a long time. The movements of your arms are in resonance with the movements of the swing. The pushes or vibrations that cause sound may be in resonance in the same way, but the movements are many times faster.

Here is a simple experiment in sound resonance. Blow across an empty pop bottle, and listen carefully to the tone the bottle makes. Ask a friend to sing the same tone. To help, blow a long tone on the bottle while your friend slides his voice up and down to find the pitch that matches. The note may be lower than you think. If the bottle is large, you may want to fill it partly with water so that it produces a tone that your friend can sing easily. Now hold the open end of the bottle close to your ear, but do not block the opening. Ask your friend to stand quite close and sing up and down the scale. Whenever he sings the note that matches the bottle's, the bottle will produce a soft tone as if you had blown gently across the top. The vibrations of the singer's vocal cords passed through the air to the

bottle. Whenever they were timed to match the natural vibrations of the air inside the bottle, the bottle produced the same tone.

Your throat, mouth, and nose cavities are called resonators, because some of the vibrations produced by your vocal cords can set the air inside the cavities into vibration. The sounds of the resonators are an important part of the quality of your voice.

SPEECH

It is said that as babies we babble all of the possible sounds used in any language. Later, as we grow up, we select the special sounds of our own language by imitation. What we call speech is simply rapid changes in the quality of vocal sound. They are made by changing the position of the lips, tongue, and velum inside the throat, mouth, and nose resonators.

35

These changes involve open-mouthed sounds and more closed sounds. An open-mouthed sound, using vibrations of the vocal cords, is called a vowel, which means *of the voice*. A sound that is closed, or noisy, is called a consonant, which means *against sound*. Still other speech sounds seem to fall partway between the vowels and the consonants.

A musical tone contains regular vibrations. When a sound contains irregular or unrelated vibrations, the result is called noise. Vowels tend to be musical, and most consonants tend to be noisy. The changes of speech are basically alternations between music and noise.

Vowels

In order to hear the vowel sounds by themselves, say them in a whisper. Simply let out a stream of air, leaving your throat open. First whisper *ah*. To make the sound of *ah,* your tongue forms a hump at the back and divides the air channel into two cavities, the mouth and the throat, leaving a narrow channel between them. The pitch of the two cavities is about the same. Your tongue forms this hump automatically when you think *ah*.

Now whisper *ay*. To form this vowel, the hump on your tongue moves up and forward toward the roof of your mouth. In this position it divides the air channel into a smaller mouth cavity and a larger throat cavity. The throat cavity now has a lower pitch, and the mouth cavity has a higher pitch. The higher sound of the mouth cavity is stronger and more noticeable.

Now whisper *ee*. To make this sound, the hump in the tongue moves even farther forward in the mouth. It leaves a still smaller front cavity behind your upper teeth and a larger cavity at the back of your throat. The back cavity sounds a very low pitch. The front cavity sounds a very high pitch, which is also stronger. Now try a long whisper sliding from *ah* through *ay* to *ee*. As the hump of your tongue moves forward, your voice passes through many vowel changes. After *ah*, it makes the vowel sound heard in *ask*, then the vowel sound *eh* as in *pet*. Next comes the vowel *ay*, then *ih* as in *pit*, ending with the vowel sound *ee*.

A second group of vowel sounds is made by changing the size of the mouth-cavity opening with the lips. Start by whispering *ah* again. Now slowly bring your lips closer together and round them at the same time. Continue whispering as you do so. Gradually your *ah* will change to *aw*, then *oh*, then the vowel sound heard in *foot*, and finally *oo* as in *boot*. By bringing your rounded lips almost together, you can make the sound of *w* as in *water*.

The sound of *y* is another partly closed sound, but it is made with the tongue instead. The tongue position for *y* is close to that for *ee*. Say *yesterday*. You will find that the *y* sound at the beginning of the word is made with the tongue in about the same forward position as it is when you make the *y* sound at the very end of the word. The tongue takes this position for only a short

38

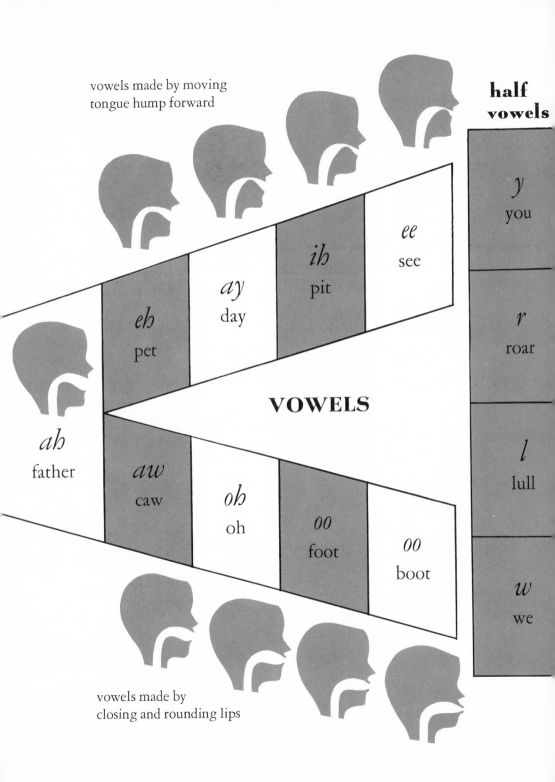

vowels made by moving
tongue hump forward

**half
vowels**

y
you

ee
see

ih
pit

ay
day

eb
pet

r
roar

VOWELS

ah
father

aw
caw

oh
oh

l
lull

oo
foot

oo
boot

w
we

vowels made by
closing and rounding lips

time whenever a person makes the *y* sound.

When you whisper you hear the vowel sounds of the resonating cavities alone. However, when you speak regularly, the source of the sounds is the vibrations of the vocal cords. The vocal vibrations also excite the air spaces in the mouth and throat cavities. The vowel sounds of the cavities are then combined with the basic sound of the vocal cords. As a result, a person may speak with either a high- or low-pitched basic tone, but the cavities sound their own pitches as the various vowel sounds, depending on the size of the cavity itself. Try holding a single tone as you change from *oo* to *oh* to *ah* to *ay* to *ee*. If you listen carefully, you can hear the vowel pitches rising gradually higher and higher.

Half Vowels

The sounds of *r* and *l* are usually called consonants. Actually they are sounds that fall between vowels and consonants, since they are vowels whose sound is changed by raising the tip of the tongue.

To produce *r*, the end of the tongue swings up toward the roof of the mouth. The tongue brushes the gums, but leaves a small space between the tip and the roof of the mouth. To make an *l* sound, the tip of the tongue touches the gum just behind the upper front teeth. The rest of the tongue sags loosely, so that there is some open space at both sides. A good *l* can also be made by touching the tip of the tongue to the upper front teeth. Along with *w* and *y*, *l* and *r* make a little group of sounds we can call half vowels.

Consonants

Some consonants are made by closing the lips. Others are made by blocking or partly blocking the mouth or throat with the tongue. Some of these sounds include sound vibrations of the vocal cords. Others are made by forcing air

41

through the small passages in the resonators.

Because consonants can be grouped in several different ways, I have arranged a simple chart on page 45. The letters in each row across are made with the mouth or tongue in the position described at the left of that row. The letters in each column running down are made according to the description at the top of that column. For instance, *p, b,* and *m* in the second row across are all made or begun with lips closed. In the same way *h, f, sh, s,* and *th,* in the first column down, are all made with a rush of air.

H Listen carefully to the consonants. The letter *h* falls in the first row and in the first column. The *h* sound is made with a stream of air rushing through an open mouth. The mouth and tongue take the position of the vowel sound that follows. Slowly say, "Ha." First there is air and then the voice vowel. Try saying, "Ho," and "Hee," and you will see that the *h* airstream is made with the mouth and tongue in position for the vowel that follows.

42

P, B, M   The letters *p, b,* and *m* each begin with lips closed and teeth slightly apart. To make the sound of *p,* air is first pushed against the closed lips, where the pressure builds up. The lips are then parted suddenly, releasing an explosion of air. To produce *b,* the vocal cords begin vibrating for a very short time while the lips are closed, making a sort of grunt. When the lips are parted, the vocal vibrations produce a vowel sound that begins as a sort of explosion. Mouth and tongue move very quickly into position for the vowel or half vowel that follows the *b.* Even at the end of a word, a short open-mouthed vowel follows the grunt of the *b.* The *b* at the end of *cab* has the sound of a quick, unaccented *buh.*

The letter *m* is voiced with the lips closed as they are when sounding *b,* but there is an important change. The velum, the muscular flap at the back of the roof of the mouth, falls forward and opens a passage into the nose. When the letters *p* and *b* are spoken, this passage is kept closed in order to trap air pressure for the explosion. Try starting a *b*, then suddenly think *m*. The velum will fall, and your vocal vibrations can now be heard through the open nose. For the best *m* sound, there should be a space between the tongue and roof of the mouth as when you make the vowel sound *ah*. The vibrations of the large mouth cavity combine with those of the throat and nose, even though the sound opening is the nose and not the mouth.

T, D, N The letters *t, d,* and *n* form a group similar to *p, b,* and *m*. But to make *t, d,* and *n* the tongue closes off the mouth opening. For *t* the edges of the tongue touch the upper teeth all around, and the tip of the tongue also touches the gum just behind the upper front teeth. This position seals off a small narrow pocket between the tongue and the roof of the mouth. The nose is closed, and air pressure is built up in the tongue pocket. When the tongue is pulled away from the teeth, an explosion of air is heard. For *d* the tongue pocket is closed in the same way. The

CONSONANTS

starting position	rush of air	blocked air	blocked voice	voice and rush of air	voice with nose open
mouth open	h				
lips closed		p	b		m
edges of tongue touch upper teeth all around		t	d		n
tongue presses against roof of mouth at back		k	g		ng
lower lip touches upper teeth	f			v	
tongue touches upper teeth at sides; wide gap at front	sh	ch	j	zh	
tongue touches upper teeth; narrow gap at front	s	ts		z	
tongue between upper and lower teeth all around	th			th	

vocal cords vibrate, making a grunt, just before the tongue pulls away from the teeth, and the grunt becomes a vowel that begins with a sort of explosion. For *n* the tongue pocket is still the same, and vocal vibrations are made with the velum dropped to open the nose. The small tongue pocket makes the *n* sound different from the *m,* which is sounded with the tongue down and lips together.

K, G, NG The letters *k, g,* and *ng* form a third consonant group. The sound *ng,* as in *sing,* is similar to that of *n.* The velum is dropped to open the nose, and the tongue forms a high hump at the back, completely cutting off the mouth cavity. Only the throat and nose resonate the vocal sound. Say *sing* and hold the *ng* at the end. Notice that your mouth is open. You should be able to close and open it again without making any change at all in the *ng* sound. The letters *k* and *g* are also made with the tongue humped at the back against the roof of the mouth, closing off the mouth completely.

The nose is also closed by the velum. Like *p* and *t,* the *k* sound is made by blocking air and releasing it in an explosion. Like *b* and *d,* the *g* sound begins with a voiced grunt, which explodes into a vowel as the tongue is released.

F, V   Notice that on the chart many of the rest of the consonants fall into two columns, one labeled "rush of air" and the other labeled "voice and rush of air." Each consonant in the first column has a companion in the other column. To sound *f,* the lower lip is placed against the upper front teeth and air is forced between. If vocal vibrations are added along with the air, the sound becomes *v.*

SH, CH,   To make *sh,* the teeth are held
ZH   close together, but not touching.
The tongue touches the upper teeth at the sides. It is close to the roof of the mouth, but leaves a flat and wide air passage at the front. There is a shallow groove in the tongue. Air rushing through this passage strikes the sharp edges of the lower front teeth. If the tongue actually

47

touches the roof of the mouth before the air is released, the explosion makes the sound of *ch.* If vocal vibrations are added to the air of *sh,* the sound becomes *zh* as in the word *azure.*

S, TS, Z The *s* sound is similar to that of *sh,* but there is only a very small opening left between the tip of the tongue and the upper front teeth. The tongue has a sharp V-shaped groove in the middle. A stream of air rushes along the narrow passage left by the groove and strikes the edge of the lower front teeth. This consonant is often the most difficult one to make, because the position must be exact. No air may be allowed to leak between tongue and teeth at the sides or into the nose. If it does, the sound becomes what is called a lisp. A child who has lost a baby tooth in the front will probably lisp an *s* sound until the new tooth grows in. Any teeth that are uneven also may make sounding a good *s* difficult.

If the *s* channel is closed, and then released with an explosion of air, the sound becomes that of *ts*. Or if vocal vibrations are added to the rushing *s* stream, the sound becomes that of *z*.

TH   One pair of consonants both have the same letter symbols—*th*. The tongue is pinched between upper and lower teeth all around, and air is forced between tongue and upper teeth. This position produces the sound of *th* in *think*. When vocal-cord vibrations are added to the rush of air, the sound becomes *th* as in *that*.

Good consonants require great flexibility of the tongue and lips. And if the tongue is not fast enough, it will not move into the best positions for the vowel sounds that come between the consonants. The velum must also respond quickly so that the nose is opened only for certain consonants and kept closed or nearly closed for all the vowels. All of these changes happen unconsciously by reflex. The quality of the speaking voice also depends on the vibrations of the vocal cords and on control of the large breathing muscles.

Tongue Twisters

Here are some tongue twisters to test your speech flexibility. Say each twister slowly, then repeat it again and again a little faster each time until you make a slip. Then start very slowly all over again. You will find that the less you think about your lips, mouth, or tongue, the more success you will have with the twisters. Simply let your jaw, lips, and tongue relax as much as possible. Your muscles will then be free to respond by reflex as you think what you want to say. If you can think the twister rapidly and clearly, the chances are good that you will say it that way.

This twister works your lips on the letter *p*. "Pat persuaded Penny to pay for Pauline's pink pajamas."

This one practices the letter *b*. "Bill bats better than Bob, but Bob is beginning to bat better."

Try your tongue on this one: "Tommy Tyler has terrible tense temper tantrums."

See if you can keep your vowels from sounding nasal in between all these *m*'s and *n*'s and *ng*'s: "My main pain is a naturally numb singing sense."

Test your *th* sound on this one: "Think things through before throwing thoughtless threats."

Here is one for the *s* and *sh* sounds: "Several sets of saddle shoes were sold at Saturday's sale."

And you can finish off with this twister to practice your sound of *k*. "Clumsy consonants can be corrected with quick concentration."

Knowledge of how the vowels and consonants are formed can help you improve your speech habits. In addition, you should learn to relax when speaking and to listen carefully to your own speech and that of others. The speech of the good speaker is automatic. Whether he is speaking at home, to a group of people, or performing in a stage play, his speaking voice projects his ideas clearly and distinctly.

SINGING

Most people like to sing or, at least, admire a pleasant singing voice. But most of us do not sound the way we would like when we open our mouth to sing. Does a person have to be born with a good voice in order to sing well? The answer is no. Singing is a fine coordination of body and brain, and so a person who has a fine natural voice without any training is most unusual. However, a person with an average or even poor-sounding voice can become pleasing to listen to with proper training.

We all have the same muscles to use for singing. And unless there is an unusual defect, even weak muscles can become strong through proper exercise. Developing these muscles depends on learning to *think* and learning to *listen*. In order to sing, you must be confident and unafraid. Your personality must let you be free to sing.

Have you ever heard a recording of your own singing voice? Most people are disappointed with what they hear, but a home tape recorder can be very useful in learning to sing. Better yet you may be able to take individual lessons with a good singing teacher. He can help you learn to hear yourself as others do. Gradually you can become a better judge of your own tones. A good teacher also can demonstrate good tones for you. Building up memories of these tones will help you decide what your own should sound like. Since you are apt to sing in the way you have learned to admire, the example of the teacher is of the greatest importance to your progress.

If you have studied piano or another instrument, you have already been training your ear to recognize pitch changes and differences in the quality of various musical sounds. The more you sharpen both your ear and your memory, the better your chance of improving your singing.

What does a good singing voice sound like? It sounds as if the tones that it produces are made without any strain, as if the high notes are sung as easily as the low notes. The voice is mellow and bright at the same time. It seems clear and is heard easily. In other words, it carries. The tones are smooth and even, resembling a well-played wind instrument, which is exactly what a good singing voice is.

How the Singing Voice Works

What happens when the singing voice is working well? First, the muscles of the face, jaw, tongue, and throat are relaxed. They are not expecting to do anything at all. A reasonably deep breath is taken with the diaphragm, and the rib cage expands gently. The lower abdominal muscles and diaphragm work against each other, producing a quick push of breath that continues in a steady flow—not too much and not too little. At the same time the mind and memory create a mental picture of the pitch, the loudness, and the quality of the tone that is wanted. The muscles in the voice box, or larynx, coordinate, stretching the vocal cords and bringing them close together as the pulse of breath arrives. The tone starts "on the breath," which means that the vocal cords are slightly open rather than tightly shut at the beginning. Then the pulse of breath sucks them together. The mental picture continues to control the muscles producing the tone as long as it lasts. Because the muscles are relaxed at the start, they are free to respond as necessary and change as the mental picture changes. Of course, the muscles work, some very hard, but the work is smooth and the action of the muscles is keenly balanced.

The process occurs by reflex. The less it is felt by the singer, the better he sounds. Most importantly, no muscles are working that are not needed.

Many things can happen to spoil this ideal state. From fear or from habit or from thought, the singer may tense muscles that interfere with good tone production. Jaw muscles may be stiff. The swallowing muscles may tighten and squeeze the throat. The tongue may be locked in place, pulling up the larynx out of its normal position at the base of the throat. The esophagus, the tube leading to the stomach, is attached at the top to some of the small muscles of the larynx. The tongue may pull up this tube, and the added weight prevents the small muscles from bringing the vocal cords together in a straight line. The throat and mouth cavities may also be too small to work as pleasant resonators.

Ideas and thoughts can be used to surprise your body into good coordination. To sigh, a person must open his throat. So sighing out the tones may prevent swallowing muscles from tightening. The brain thinks, Sigh, as the tone starts. Pretending you are about to yawn as you begin to sing may accomplish the same thing. Thinking, Oh well, may let your tongue and jaw muscles relax enough to respond as they should. Sometimes pretending that you are not singing at all is a help. You imagine that you are listen-

Profile of poor singing tone. Lips, tongue, and jaw tense. Larynx pulled too high. Throat and mouth too small.

Profile of good singing tone. Lips and tongue flexible. Jaw relaxed. Larynx remains lower. Larger mouth, longer throat.

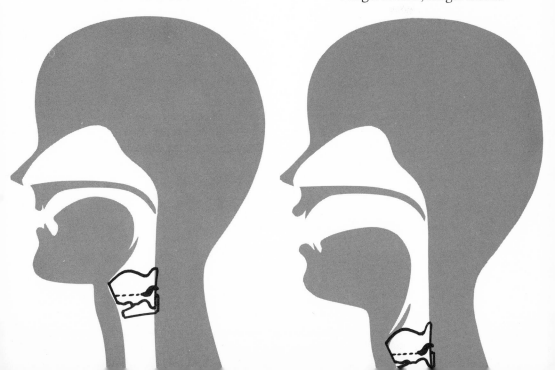

ing to the tone and that it is being sung with great ease. Sometimes thinking of the kind of tone you would like to hear is useful. On the other hand, if you pretend you don't care at all what the tone sounds like, you may get the best sound of all.

Breath Control

The muscles that are safest to pay attention to are the large breathing muscles, the diaphragm and the abdominals. You do have some conscious control over them. Working with them can steady the flow of breath and keep the rest of the small muscles responding only as they are needed.

Here are some simple exercises that can help you with breath control. First, lie down on your back without a pillow. Place your hands gently on your stomach just below the waist. Let yourself breathe easily, and feel the movement as you inhale. Let yourself exhale gently. Notice that you seem to be expanding and relaxing below your chest. Remain lying down. Raise your rib cage a little, and hold it in an easy, expanded position. Let your shoulders fall. Breathe in as before, feeling the expansion in your abdominal muscles. Now tighten your abdominal muscles a little, but hold your breath as you do so. Keep this low firm feeling and exhale slowly saying "Ssssss" like a leaky tire. Listen to make sure that the *s* sound stays smooth and even. Feel as though you are lifting the breath firmly up through your expanded rib cage. At the end of the breath think about keeping the rib cage from collapsing.

When the breath is controlled firmly in this way, the vocal cords are free to respond without being forced to hold back too much breath pres-

inhale

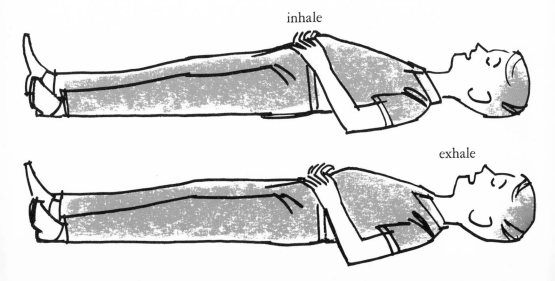

exhale

sure. Now stand straight, but relaxed. Use the same breath control you used for the *s* exercise, but let yourself sing "Ah" instead. Start the *ah* with a gentle push of your abdominal muscles. Try a pitch in about the middle of your voice. Now practice changing gradually from *ah* to *oh*. Simply think, Ah—oh, and pretend that your throat is resting comfortably, as if you might

inhale   exhale

THE SINGER'S BREATH

Chest is gently expanded. Diaphragm tightens and flattens. Abdominals tighten in opposition. A bulge appears below rib cage. Diaphragm relaxes gradually as abdominals increase tension. Stomach flattens as breath is exhaled. Chest feels expanded as at first until a new breath is taken.

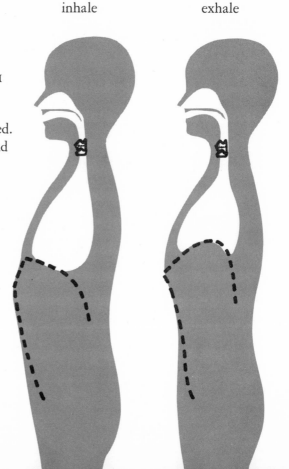

begin to yawn at any time. Now move from *ah* to *ay* gently. Then begin again and move from *ah* to *ee*. You may make some progress by yourself, but you will make more with a teacher. The teacher is like a doctor. He can diagnose your particular faults and give you exercises to overcome your special problems.

Voice Ranges

Voices are pitched high or low depending on the length and thickness of the vocal cords. Longer or thicker cords produce lower notes easily. Shorter or thinner cords produce higher notes easily. Voices are grouped according to the range of pitches that they can sing. The diagram shows these ranges on the piano keyboard. The lowest voice is called bass. The next is baritone, which is the most common range for a man, and the highest man's voice is tenor. Alto is the lowest woman's voice, mezzo soprano is next, and soprano is the highest. Notice that each range covers two octaves, or two do-re-mi scales. These ranges are not exact, and every individual voice has its own particular range. Voices of boys and girls who have not reached puberty usually fall in the mezzo soprano range.

Children's voices are usually light in quality and often a little breathy. The breathy sound is caused by the vocal cords not being brought close enough together or not being closed completely at the back. The arytenoid cartilages can rock to bring the flexible edges of the cords together, but still leave an open chink just behind. Then some extra breath rushes through the chink while the cords are vibrating. This characteristic is typical of young or untrained voices. Usually the air gap disappears as the voice is used more and more. Trying to produce a tone that is not breathy before the muscles have become strong enough may be harmful. A boy or girl who sings easily with a light tone will gradually develop a stronger one.

Young boys sometimes think that they must

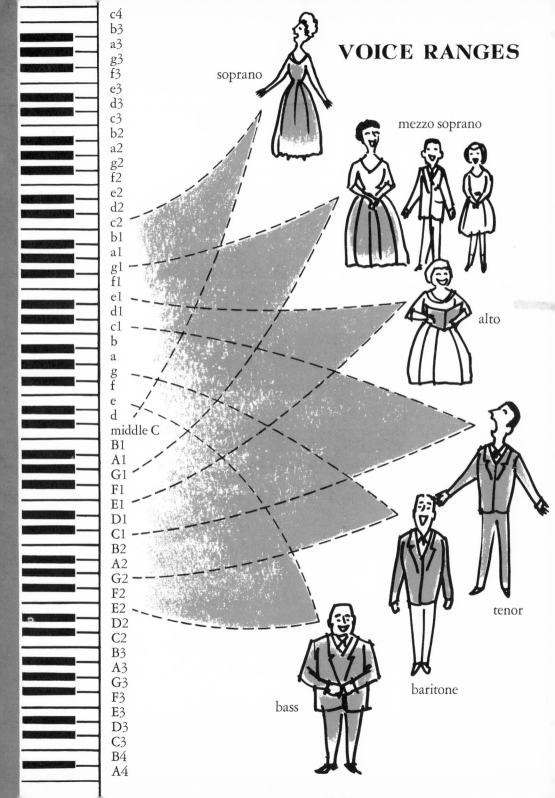

VOICE RANGES

soprano

mezzo soprano

alto

tenor

baritone

bass

c4
b3
a3
g3
f3
e3
d3
c3
b2
a2
g2
f2
e2
d2
c2
b1
a1
g1
f1
e1
d1
c1
b
a
g
f
e
d
middle C
B1
A1
G1
F1
E1
D1
C1
B2
A2
G2
F2
E2
D2
C2
B3
A3
G3
F3
E3
D3
C3
B4
A4

sound low and deep rather than high and silly like the girls. But before it changes the range of a boy's voice may be as high or higher than that of a girl's, and it should be used in its natural range. Often children singing in a group make tones that are a combination of loud talking or shouting and singing. Usually a person speaks in the lower part of his singing range. If singing is forced loudly in this range, some of the muscles in the larynx may tend to lock in fixed positions. Then they are not able to adjust naturally for each change of pitch. A person singing this way may never discover how to produce the true high tones in his range. A voice that is free and flexible may not sound as loud at first, but the tones will be musical and the range will be greater. And the voice will gain in clarity and volume with practice.

How Voices Carry

You may have noticed that some singing voices

seem to carry well, even in a large room, while others sound dull, even at a short distance. Part of the reason lies in the voice and part in the ear that hears the sounds. Like any air cavity, the tube leading into the eardrum has its own resonant pitch. And the membrane of the eardrum is set into vibration more easily when certain pitches are produced.

When you listen to a singing tone, you notice most of all the pitch that is sung. But you also hear a certain color or quality in the tone, because the vocal vibrations really produce a whole group of pitches at once. They are called overtones, since each one is over, or higher than, the ones below. The slowest vibrations are called the fundamental. You hear them as the pitch note of the tone. Vibrations that are twice as frequent form the first overtone, one octave above. Vibrations that are three times as fast form the second overtone, five do-re-mi steps above the first. Still higher overtones fall even closer together. A soft or dull tone may have only a few overtones that are strong enough to hear. A rich, ringing tone has many—high as well as low. The ear hears best the pitches around 3000 vibrations per second. If the vocal tone includes a strong overtone close to this pitch, the tone will be heard very easily. Such a tone is made to fit the ear.

If you can whistle a very high pitch, you will find that your tongue makes a small pocket behind your front teeth of about the size it makes for the vowel sound *ee*. The high pitch of *ee* is around 3000 vibrations per second, so that if you are speaking or singing "Ee" it sounds more penetrating than the other vowels. By coincidence this pitch is close to that of the highest E on the piano keyboard. A voice that carries has some of this *ee* pitch almost all of the time.

But where does this pitch come from when other vowels are used? The answer is that there are small natural cavities that may also resonate this pitch. Between the true vocal cord and false vocal cord on each side is a small cavity. These cavities may help to resonate the *ee* pitch that carries so well. Also, behind each pillar, or muscle flap, holding up the arch of the velum is a small cavity that may be adjusted to help resonate the *ee* pitch. Which of these small cavities are most important is not certain. But if a singer has a clear tone in mind, and if his vocal cords are producing the needed vibrations, the resonant cavities will respond if they are relaxed and flexible.

A singing voice can be bright or ringing and also mellow or deep at the same time. Suppose the vocal vibrations are rich with overtones. Small cavities emphasize the highest overtones, while larger mouth or throat cavities emphasize lower overtones.

A small, tense throat can emphasize high overtones but not the low. Such tones are shrill. A throat that is open but too tense may emphasize low overtones, while the small resonators are not able to adjust properly for the higher overtones. Such a voice is deep but muffled. Only as all the muscles of mouth and throat are free and flexible, can they adjust to resonate both high and low overtones at once. The voices we like best to hear are those that have the greatest contrast between high and low overtones and a good balance between them.

Vibrato

Another quality that is present in good singing voices is called vibrato. Your nervous system has several control centers. Each center sends messages to muscles at its own special rate. When you are cold and shiver, messages are being sent to your muscles about twenty times per second, and your teeth chatter at that speed. Your highest brain center sends messages regularly about ten times per second. When this brain pulse controls some of the muscles used in singing, they tense and relax about six or seven times each second. In between they have time to relax only a little before working again. Still, this short rest six or seven times each second means that the muscles can continue to do strong work much more easily than if they remained tense all of the time. The result is a natural pulsebeat in the singing tone. With each complete pulse the pitch rises and falls a little, and at the same time the sound grows louder and softer. Usually the carrying overtone is produced only during the strongest part of the pulse, so that it jingles like a tiny bell. Then the voice truly rings. These pulse changes come fast enough so that the ear does not notice them separately. Instead, we seem to hear a beautiful singing tone that is rich and pleasant.

The muscles of young or untrained singers usually do not work as vigorously. As a result, there are no on-and-off pulses; the tone sounds very smooth and simple. However, a voice that is used well will gain in muscular strength, and gradually an even and regular vibrato will develop.

You can make a crude imitation of the vibrato by blowing up a balloon. Pinch the neck and let

some air escape. As the collapsing balloon produces vibrations in the neck, move your hands
slowly a little farther apart and a little closer
together. Gradually speed up the movement. If
you can move them back and forth about six or
seven times per second, you will produce a
balloon vibrato. The balloon is likely to sound
like a wobbly soprano who is having some
trouble staying on pitch. With practice you can
make the pulses more regular, and the effect will
be that of a more even tone. In the same way a
voice whose pulses are timed precisely and are

timing the balloon vibrato
at 6 or 7 times per second

very regular produces a tone that is more alive and pleasant. The vibrato of the singing voice is an unconscious part of all the reflex muscular actions. To a good singer the best tones are made with almost no conscious feelings at all.

VENTRILOQUISM

A ventriloquist is a person who can manufacture voices other than his own and make them seem to come from somewhere else. Sometimes he makes a dummy speak in a high squeaky voice. Sometimes he produces a voice that sounds trapped in a box or in a closet or as if someone were shouting from a distance. The voice may even sound as if it were coming over a telephone. This kind of voice magic is fun for everyone in the audience. For the ventriloquist, especially at first, it is a lot of very hard work.

The word *ventriloquism* comes from two Latin words meaning *belly speech*. It was once thought that the ventriloquist's sounds originated in the stomach. Instead, the ventriloquist makes them with skillful use of his ordinary vocal apparatus. But the belly is still important, because ventriloquism requires some of the same breath control that is used for singing. The diaphragm and abdominals work much more vigorously in this kind of speaking than they do in ordinary speech.

The secrets of the ventriloquist can be learned by anyone, but time, patience, and concentration are needed to master them. Much depends on very careful listening and thinking. The ventriloquist must develop some new speech habits and the ability to switch back and forth between the new ones and the old. Often he speaks for at least two people—himself and the dummy he pretends to be. This ability takes a sort of split mental control, which must be developed gradually. At the same time the ventriloquist usually operates a dummy something like a hand puppet, and his actions must be perfectly timed with the dummy's speech. These skills are a lot to learn, but they are certainly worth the effort. If you are really interested, you can become a pretty good ventriloquist.

I was not a ventriloquist before writing this book, so I had to learn just as you will. Here are some of the steps that were most helpful to me.

Silent Lips, Flexible Tongue

Whatever voice he manufactures, the ventriloquist wants it to sound as if it comes from somewhere else. We all move our lips and jaws when we speak. Sometimes we guess what a person says by watching his mouth even though we cannot hear the sounds. So the first job of the ventriloquist is to learn to speak clearly without moving anything that can be seen from the outside.

Start by bringing your teeth gently together, but do not tighten your jaw. Part your lips about wide enough so that the tip of your first finger will slide between them. Smiling a little may help. Stand in front of a mirror so that you can watch for any telltale mouth movements. In your normal voice sound the vowels *ee, ay, ah, oh, oo.* Since your lips and lower jaw cannot move, all of the changes for these vowels must be made by the tongue. Don't think about your tongue, however. Listen to yourself speak these vowels as if someone else in the room were saying them. Imagine that they are going to sound just as they do in ordinary speech. If your mouth and tongue feel relaxed, your tongue will automatically find the best positions for the vowels.

You may notice that when you say the vowels *ah, oh,* and *oo,* your tongue feels pulled down lower than usual. Because your lower jaw cannot drop, the tongue alone must drop to make a large enough mouth cavity for these vowels to sound. This movement will happen properly if you *think* what you want to hear. Thinking of the sounds as being right on the tip of the tongue or out in front of your teeth is also helpful. Imagine that everything you say is extra crisp and clear. Remember that your teeth need to touch slightly in order to hide your tongue movements. Probably you will find that the vowels are not too hard to say.

Difficult Consonants

Review again the consonants on the next page. Try saying each of them with your lips parted and teeth gently touching. You will find that most of these sounds, like the vowels, can be spoken with little or no difficulty. However, five of them—*p, b, m, f,* and *v*—are a real problem. The letters *p, b,* and *m* all start with lips closed. The letters *f* and *v* are made with the lower lip

CONSONANTS

starting position	rush of air	blocked air	blocked voice	voice and rush of air	voice with nose open
mouth open	*h*				
lips closed		*p*	*b*		*m*
edges of tongue touch upper teeth all around		*t*	*d*		*n*
tongue presses against roof of mouth at back		*k*	*g*		*ng*
lower lip touches upper teeth	*f*			*v*	
tongue touches upper teeth at sides; wide gap at front	*sh*	*ch*	*j*	*zh*	
tongue touches upper teeth; narrow gap at front	*s*	*ts*		*z*	
tongue between upper and lower teeth all around	*th*			*th*	

touching the upper teeth. How are these sounds going to be made without moving the lips? Although sounding them absolutely perfectly may seem impossible, it can be done. The answer is that one imitates the *sounds* of these consonants rather than their positions. The ventriloquist learns to make a consonant formed with the tongue sound just like a consonant formed with the lips.

Look again at the consonant chart. The letters *p, b,* and *m* are all in the same row across. Just below them in the next row are the consonants *t, d,* and *n.* For *t, d,* and *n* the tongue touches the upper teeth all around, making a small pocket below the roof of the mouth and preventing sound from coming out the mouth. For *p, b,* and *m* the tongue is low in the mouth, leaving a larger mouth cavity, and the lips block the opening. The cause of the difference in the sounds of these two groups of consonants is not so much what blocks the opening but the size of the mouth cavity. The secret of making *t, d,* and *n* sound like *p, b,* and *m* is to increase the size of the tongue pocket.

First say the sound of *n* with lips parted and teeth gently together. Listen very carefully. Now let your tongue sag as if it is very heavy, but do not let the edges and tip pull away from the upper teeth. This position makes the tongue pocket larger, and the sound is more like that of *m*. Think *m* as you let your tongue sag. Gradually you can develop a better and better imitation. *Mom* is a good word to practice very slowly.

Try the *b* next. First say, "Dee," and notice the small space between tongue and roof of mouth as you start the consonant. Let your tongue sag down and forward toward your front teeth, but do not let the edges and tip pull away from the upper teeth. You will form a larger tongue pocket, and the *d* will change to *b*. *Bob* is a good word to practice very slowly.

The letter *p* is a little harder to produce, but the principle is the same. First say the letter *t*. Notice that you release an explosion of air when making this sound. Let the tongue pocket sag down and forward, and the air exploding becomes a *p*. *Pop* is a good practice word. Don't rush. Go very slowly, listen carefully, and think what you want to hear.

The remaining difficult consonants are *f* and *v,* which form a pair. Both are normally made with the lower lip touching the upper front teeth. The letter *f* is made by forcing air between the lower lip and teeth. The letter *v* is made in the same way, but vocal vibrations are added to the rush of air. The ventriloquist must make these consonants with the tongue alone while lips are parted and teeth are held together. The closest tongue consonant in sound is that of *th*. It is made normally with the tongue pinched between the upper and lower teeth all around, and it is really a pair of sounds. The first is made by forcing air between tongue and upper teeth. The second is made in the same way with the addition of vocal vibrations.

You have already discovered that you can make

a good *th* sound with your tongue pressed behind your teeth rather than pinched between them. The fact that the sound of *f* is very much like the sound of *th* is also helpful. First make each sound in the normal way and listen very carefully. Notice that the rush of air for the *f* sound seems a little lower and duller than that for the *th*. You can turn a *th* into an *f* simply by relaxing the pressure of your tongue against the teeth a little. The difference is slight and must be quite exact. If you learn to hear the difference between the normal *th* and *f,* your ear and memory will guide your imitation. Once you have mastered the *f* you can turn it into a *v* by adding vocal vibrations to the rush of air.

The Drone Voice

The next step is to develop a voice sound that is quite different from your own. It can be lower or higher. Usually the higher voice is easier to produce and seems more appropriate to the small

dummies that most ventriloquists use. The basic
tone for this high voice is called the drone. It is
a penetrating buzz, or hum, which sounds something like a bumblebee. It is also something like
a whine or a siren. When you make the drone,
you feel small and squeezed, as if you are not
letting out much breath.

First do an imitation of a fire siren rising and
falling. Now in a voice that feels higher and
smaller than your own say, "Zee, zee, zee, zee,
zeeeeee," and hold the final *ee* sound. The idea is
to get a penetrating buzzy sort of *ee*. If you put
your hands on your stomach, you will find that
you are using your large breathing muscles to
control a very firm breath stream. At the same
time you seem to be holding back so as not to
let out too much breath at once. The result is
that your voice box is higher than usual, making
your voice sound smaller than usual. The buzzy
sound means that your vocal cords are held together more firmly than usual. To keep this sound
going all of the time you are speaking takes some

concentration at first. Later the ability will become a habit. In the beginning you should practice only for short periods in order to give your voice plenty of rest while the muscles get used to the new way of working. Be very patient.

Now you are ready to combine the small voice with the new positions you have learned for sounding the difficult consonants—lips parted and teeth touching gently all the time. A good exercise is to stand before a mirror and very slowly pronounce the names of all the letters of the alphabet using the ventriloquist's voice. In this way you can practice many of the sound combinations that you will need to learn. Let your ear be the final judge.

Distant Voices

Once you have found the drone voice, you can try other voice imitations. Have a friend step inside a closet and call out to you. Listen to the special muffled quality of the closet voice. Then try imitating this quality using your drone voice. Your tongue will hump back to close off your throat partly as you mimic this sound.

The same basic technique is used to imitate voices calling from a distance. Again you must listen to the real sounds to build up a memory of the quality. Notice that only the highest pitches carry and that the consonants are lost completely if the distance is great enough.

To imitate the voice coming out of the ear-

piece of a telephone receiver, you must use a similar method. In this case the pitches are not quite as high, because the voice is speaking and not shouting. There is a peculiar distortion in the phone voice. Lower frequencies do not carry, and the voice seems to be squeezed out through a narrow slot. It may also sound a little nasal or twangy. If you can get a willing friend to take the time to call you up, listen to his voice with the receiver held out away from your ear. Ear and memory will control your imitations.

Routine with a Dummy

Of course, a ventriloquist needs a dummy and a routine. Some of the dummies are quite complicated in construction. However, here is one that you can always rig up quickly to have some fun. You need only a small brown paper bag. Fold the bag flat with the bottom facing you. The folded bottom forms a flap that you can use

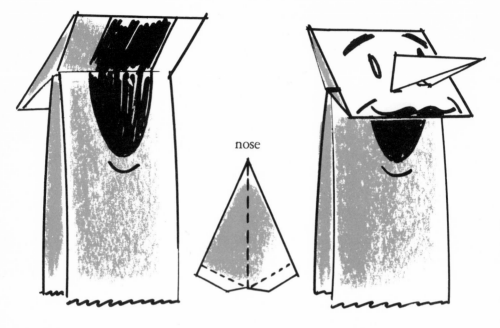

nose

paper-bag dummy

for a mouth. Paint eyes and upper lip on the
bottom flap. Glue on a nose made from folded
paper. Paint the rest of the mouth on the side of
the bag under the bottom flap, so that a lower lip
shows when the mouth is closed. You can also
paint a shirt or dress on the lower part of the bag.
Slip your hand into the bag, and curl your fingers

over into the bottom flap. By raising and lowering the tips of your fingers, the dummy's mouth will seem to open and close.

First practice coordinating your ventriloquist's voice with the mouth movements of the dummy. Then practice switching from the puppet's voice to your normal voice. Go slowly and make the switches very definite. Your own voice should sound low and relaxed, and the dummy's should sound high and penetrating. In order to create the effect that two people are having a conversa-

tion, you must practically convince yourself that you *are* two people at once.

It is fun to make up your own routines and use your own ideas, but here is a short one you can practice to get started.

Ventriloquist: What's your name?

Bag Puppet: Just call me Phil.

Ventriloquist: Phil who?

Bag Puppet: Phil the bag.

Ventriloquist: Fill the bag! That sounds pretty funny.

Bag Puppet: You'd sound funny too if your voice came out of a sack.

Ventriloquist: Do you work?

Bag Puppet: Only when you do.

Ventriloquist: No, I don't mean that. I mean do you have a job?

Bag Puppet: Yes, I do.

Ventriloquist: What is it?

Bag Puppet: I don't know if I should tell you.

Ventriloquist: Why not?

Bag Puppet: You'll laugh.

Ventriloquist: Tell me *where* you work.

Bag Puppet: At the supermarket.

Ventriloquist: Well, what is your job at the supermarket?

Bag Puppet: I carry out groceries!

Ventriloquist: Is *that* what you call a good joke?

Bag Puppet: Well, I thought *that* joke was in the *bag*!

This routine does not avoid the difficult consonants. If you give them enough practice, your dummy will be able to say anything he wants to. Your job is to make speaking easy for him.

Whatever you do or wherever you go, your voice goes with you. It lets others know what you think and feel. Your voice tells who you really are. Your voice is you.

Glossary of Terms

abdominals, a group of muscles at the front and sides of the trunk, which connect the rib cage to the pelvis.

Adam's apple, protruding wedge in neck where the thyroid shields meet at the front of the voice box.

arytenoid cartilages, two ladle-shaped cartilages attached to the vocal cords at the back of the voice box. They separate to move the vocal cords apart or meet to bring the cords together.

breath control, opposition of the diaphragm and abdominal muscles, which creates a firm and smooth flow of breath for speech or singing.

bronchi, two tubes that form an upside down Y and connect the trachea to each lung.

consonant, a speech noise made by blocking or partly blocking vocal sound.

cricoid ring, the signet-shaped ring of cartilage, at the top of the trachea, that forms the base of the voice box.

diaphragm, the muscular divider that separates rib cage and lungs from the lower body organs.

drone, a high and penetrating buzzlike tone used by a ventriloquist as a basis for voice imitations.

esophagus, throat tube, behind the trachea, that carries food to the stomach.

false vocal cords, two small muscular shelves that lie just above the true vocal cords, forming tiny pockets on either side of the throat.

half vowel, a speech sound that is not as open as a vowel or as closed as a consonant. *Y, w, l,* and *r* can be called half vowels.

larynx, the voice box, formed by the cricoid ring and the thyroid shields, which contains the vocal cords.

noise, a sound made by vibrations that are irregular or unrelated.

overtone, one of the series of related vibrations in a musical tone, each one over or higher in pitch than those below.

pharynx, the vertical section of throat above the voice box.

reflex, any automatic muscular reaction that occurs without conscious control.

resonance, the natural vibrations of an object or cavity stimulated by another object vibrating at that same frequency.

ring, the carrying quality in a voice produced by a strong overtone around 3000 cycles per second.

singing, the sounds of speech prolonged and adapted to a fixed series of pitch intervals.

speech, specific alternations between music and noise used in vocal communication.

thyroid cartilage, a double shield of cartilage, open at the back and joined at the front, that forms the largest part of the voice box.

tone (musical), sound produced by vibrations that are related and regular.

trachea, the windpipe below the larynx.

velum, arch-shaped muscular flap at the back of the roof of the mouth.

ventriloquism, the skillful use of one's vocal apparatus to imitate sounds coming from another source.

vibration, any rapid and continuous back and forth motion.

vibrato, the muscular on and off pulse in a voice that occurs regularly six or seven times per second and makes the voice sound "live."

vocal cords, wedge-shaped shelves of muscle in the larynx that can be brought together and vibrated by a stream of breath.

vowel, a speech sound made by vocal vibrations resonated in an open mouth and throat.

Index

indicates illustration

94